*Simple & Delicious*

# BAKING

# *Simple & Delicious*
# BAKING

OVER 100 SENSATIONAL RECIPES FOR BAKING CLASSICS

This edition published in 2012
LOVE FOOD is an imprint of Parragon Books Ltd

Parragon
Chartist House
15-17 Trim Street
Bath BA1 1HA, UK
www.parragon.com

ISBN: 978-1-4454-8263-7

Printed in China

Cover Design by Geoff Borin
Additional Photography by Clive Bozzard-Hill
Additional Food Styling by Valerie Barrett and Carol Tennant

Notes for the Reader
This book uses both metric and imperial measurements. Follow the same units of measurement throughout; do not mix metric and imperial. All spoon measurements are level: teaspoons are assumed to be 5 ml, and tablespoons are assumed to be 15 ml. Unless otherwise stated, milk is assumed to be full fat, eggs and individual vegetables are medium, and pepper is freshly ground black pepper. Unless otherwise stated, all root vegetables should be washed and peeled prior to using.

Garnishes, decorations and serving suggestions are all optional and not necessarily included in the recipe ingredients or method.

The times given are an approximate guide only. Preparation times differ according to the techniques used by different people and the cooking times may also vary from those given. Optional ingredients, variations or serving suggestions have not been included in the time calculations.

Recipes using raw or very lightly cooked eggs should be avoided by infants, the elderly, pregnant women, convalescents and anyone suffering from an illness. Pregnant and breastfeeding women are advised to avoid eating peanuts and peanut products. Sufferers from nut allergies should be aware that some of the ready-made ingredients used in the recipes in this book may contain nuts. Always check the packaging before use.

# Contents

# Introduction

Baking is just about the most rewarding and enjoyable type of cooking there is. Perhaps it's down to the tantalizing aroma of cakes and cookies as they emerge from the oven, the satisfaction of cutting into a freshly baked cake or the delight in presenting family and friends with an elaborate home-made dessert for a special occasion. Whatever the reason, it's never too late too discover the pleasures of baking.

With our hectic lifestyles, many of us feel that we simply don't have the time for home-baking, but this book shows that you don't have to spend hours in the kitchen to achieve worthwhile results. Many of the recipes will take as little as half an hour of your time, and even the more elaborate creations are easily accessible to the novice cook thanks to the easy-to-follow instructions and clear ingredients lists. What's more, each recipe is illustrated with a beautiful colour photograph of the finished dish, which should be just enough incentive to get you into the kitchen for a baking session!

From homely pies and tarts to delicious muffins and cookies, and from simple sponge cakes to stylish gateaux, this book is packed with recipes to suit all tastes and every occasion, whatever your skill level. The recipes are divided into four sections – Cakes, Slices & Bars, Cookies & Small Cakes, and Desserts – making it simple to find the recipe you need. There are delectable cakes to enjoy at any time of the day, mouth-watering cookies to accompany your afternoon cuppa and bite-sized cupcakes that are perfect for the children's lunch boxes, plus many more tempting treats to delight all the family.

All the instructions you will need are included in the recipes so, provided you follow them carefully, you really cannot go wrong. Nevertheless, the following hints and tips should be beneficial for both beginner and more experienced cooks and will help to ensure perfect results every time.

• Always read the recipe through carefully and measure out the ingredients before you start cooking.

• When measuring out ingredients, follow the same units of measurement throughout – either metric or imperial. For small amounts, use a set of standard measuring spoons and smooth the contents level for accuracy.

• Preheat the oven to the specified temperature. This usually takes about

15 minutes (depending on your oven) and the recipe will indicate the appropriate stage.

• Avoiding opening the oven during cooking, especially if you are baking a delicate cake. If you cannot resist taking a peek, wait until at least halfway through the cooking time. If the cake is becoming a little too dark, but is not yet cooked through, cover loosely with foil to prevent the top from burning.

• It is important to use the cake tin specified in the recipe. If you don't have the correct-sized cake tin, at least use a tin with the same volume. For example, a 20-cm/8-inch round cake tin has approximately the same capacity as an 18-cm/7-inch square cake tin.

• For most recipes (except pastry), fats should be used at room temperature for ease of mixing. It's also a good idea to remove eggs from the refrigerator 30 minutes before you start to mix.

• To melt chocolate, either on its own or with other ingredients, place in a heatproof bowl set over a pan of gently simmering (not boiling) water and stir until melted. Make sure that the base of the bowl does not touch the water.

• To test cakes for doneness, press the surface lightly with your finger. It should feel springy to the touch; if your finger leaves an indent, the cake is not yet ready. Alternatively, test by inserting a skewer into the centre of the cake – it should come out clean. Brownies should be cooked until they are firm to the touch and a crust has formed on the surface, but should still be slightly gooey inside. Biscuits should be baked until evenly coloured and firm to the touch.

• Cakes and biscuits can be stored in an airtight container at room temperature, unless they have a filling or fresh cream icing in which case they should be stored in the refrigerator. Make sure that they have cooled completely before storing.

# Cakes

# Victoria Sponge Cake

*serves 8–10*

175 g/6 oz butter, softened,
plus extra for greasing

175 g/6 oz caster sugar

3 eggs, beaten

175 g/6 oz self-raising flour

pinch of salt

3 tbsp raspberry jam

1 tbsp caster or icing sugar

Preheat the oven to 180°C/350°F/Gas Mark 4. Grease two 20-cm/8-inch sandwich tins and line the bases with baking paper.

Cream the butter and sugar together in a mixing bowl using a wooden spoon or a hand-held mixer until the mixture is pale in colour and light and fluffy.

Add the egg a little at a time, beating well after each addition. Sift the flour and salt and carefully add to the mixture, folding it in with a metal spoon or a spatula.

Divide the mixture between the prepared tins and smooth over with the spatula.

Place them on the same shelf in the centre of the preheated oven and bake for 25–30 minutes, until well risen, golden brown and beginning to shrink from the sides of the tin.

Remove from the oven and allow to cool slightly. Loosen the cakes from around the edge of the tins using a palette knife. Turn the cakes out onto a clean tea towel, remove the paper and invert them onto a wire rack.

When completely cool, sandwich the cakes together with the jam and sprinkle the top with the sugar.

# Chocolate Fudge Cake

*serves 8*

175 g/6 oz unsalted butter, softened, plus extra for greasing

175 g/6 oz golden caster sugar

3 eggs, beaten

3 tbsp golden syrup

40 g/1½ oz ground almonds

175 g/6 oz self-raising flour

pinch of salt

40 g/1½ oz cocoa powder

*icing*

225 g/8 oz plain chocolate, broken into pieces

55 g/2 oz dark muscovado sugar

225 g/8 oz unsalted butter, diced

5 tbsp evaporated milk

½ tsp vanilla extract

Grease two 20-cm/8-inch sandwich tins and line the bases with baking paper.

To make the icing, place the chocolate, muscovado sugar, butter, evaporated milk and vanilla extract in a heavy-based saucepan. Heat gently, stirring constantly, until melted. Pour into a bowl and leave to cool. Cover and chill in the refrigerator for 1 hour, or until spreadable.

Preheat the oven to 180°C/350°F/Gas Mark 4. Place the butter and caster sugar in a bowl and beat together until light and fluffy. Gradually beat in the eggs. Stir in the golden syrup and ground almonds. Sift the flour, salt and cocoa powder into a separate bowl, then fold into the mixture. Add a little water, if necessary, to make a dropping consistency.

Spoon the mixture into the prepared tins and bake in the preheated oven for 30–35 minutes, or until springy to the touch and a skewer inserted in the centre comes out clean.

Leave the cakes in the tins for 5 minutes, then turn out onto wire racks to cool completely. When the cakes are cold, sandwich them together with half the icing. Spread the remaining icing over the top and sides of the cake.

# Coffee Streusel Cake

*serves 8–10*

225 g/8 oz plain flour

1 tbsp baking powder

70 g/2½ oz caster sugar

150 ml/5 fl oz milk

2 eggs

115 g/4 oz butter, melted and cooled, plus extra for greasing

2 tbsp instant coffee granules, dissolved in 1 tbsp boiling water

50 g/1¾ oz chopped almonds

icing sugar, for dusting

*topping*

70 g/2½ oz self-raising flour

70 g/2½ oz demerara sugar

2 tbsp butter, cut into small pieces

1 tsp ground mixed spice

Preheat the oven to 190°C/375°F/Gas Mark 5. Grease a 23-cm/9-inch loose-based round cake tin and line with baking paper.

Sift the plain flour and baking powder into a mixing bowl, then stir in the caster sugar.

Whisk the milk, eggs, melted butter and coffee mixture together and pour onto the dry ingredients. Add the chopped almonds and mix lightly together. Spoon the mixture into the prepared tin.

To make the topping, mix the self-raising flour and demerara sugar together in a bowl. Rub in the butter with your fingertips until the mixture resembles breadcrumbs. Sprinkle in the mixed spice and 1 tablespoon of water and bring the mixture together in loose crumbs. Sprinkle the topping evenly over the cake.

Bake in the preheated oven for 50 minutes–1 hour. Cover loosely with foil if the topping starts to brown too quickly.

Leave to cool in the tin. Remove the cake from the tin and dust with icing sugar just before serving.

# Chocolate & Walnut Cake

serves 8

4 eggs

125 g/4½ oz caster sugar

75 g/2¾ oz plain chocolate, broken into pieces

125 g/4½ oz plain flour

1 tbsp cocoa powder

2 tbsp butter, melted, plus extra for greasing

115 g/4 oz walnuts, finely chopped

walnut halves, to decorate

### icing

75 g/2¾ oz plain chocolate

115 g/4 oz butter

175 g/6 oz icing sugar

2 tbsp milk

Preheat the oven to 160°C/325°F/Gas Mark 3. Grease an 18-cm/7-inch deep round cake tin and line with baking paper.

Place the eggs and caster sugar in a bowl and whisk with an electric whisk for 10 minutes, or until foamy and a trail is left when the whisk is dragged across the surface. Put the chocolate in a heatproof bowl set over a saucepan of gently simmering water until melted.

Sift the flour and cocoa together and fold into the egg and sugar mixture with a spoon or a palette knife. Fold in the melted butter, melted chocolate and chopped walnuts. Pour into the prepared tin and bake in the preheated oven for 30–35 minutes, or until springy to the touch.

Leave to cool in the tin for 5 minutes, then transfer to a wire rack and leave to cool completely.

To make the icing, melt the chocolate as above and leave to cool slightly. Beat together the butter, icing sugar and milk until the mixture is pale and fluffy. Whisk in the melted chocolate.

Cut the cake into 2 layers of equal thickness. Place the bottom half on a serving plate, spread with some of the icing and put the other half on top. Spread the remaining icing over the top of the cake with a palette knife. Decorate with walnut halves and serve.

# Carrot & Ginger Cake

*serves* 10

butter, for greasing

280 g/10 oz plain flour

1 tsp baking powder

1 tsp bicarbonate of soda

2 tsp ground ginger

½ tsp salt

175 g/6 oz dark muscovado sugar

325 g/11½ oz grated carrots

2 pieces chopped stem ginger

1 tbsp grated fresh ginger

55 g/2 oz raisins

2 eggs, beaten

3 tbsp sunflower oil

juice of 1 orange

strips of orange zest, to decorate

*icing*

225 g/8 oz cream cheese

4 tbsp icing sugar

1 tsp vanilla extract

Preheat the oven to 180°C/350°F/Gas Mark 4. Grease a 20-cm/8-inch round cake tin and line with baking paper.

Sift the flour, baking powder, bicarbonate of soda, ground ginger and salt into a bowl. Stir in the muscovado sugar, carrots, stem ginger, fresh ginger and raisins. Beat together the eggs, oil and orange juice, then pour into the bowl with the dry ingredients. Mix together well.

Spoon the mixture into the prepared tin and bake in the preheated oven for 1–1¼ hours, until firm to the touch and a skewer inserted into the centre of the cake comes out clean. Leave to cool in the tin.

To make the icing, place the cream cheese in a bowl and beat to soften. Sift in the icing sugar and add the vanilla extract. Mix well.

Remove the cake from the tin and spread the icing over the top. Decorate the cake with strips of orange zest and serve.

# Cherry & Almond Cake

*serves 8*

300 g/10½ oz glacé cherries

175 g/6 oz butter, softened, plus extra for greasing

175 g/6 oz golden caster sugar

3 eggs

40 g/1½ oz ground almonds

280 g/10 oz plain flour

1½ tsp baking powder

70 g/2½ oz flaked almonds

Preheat the oven to 160°C/325°F/Gas Mark 3. Grease an 18-cm/7-inch square cake tin and line with baking paper.

Cut the cherries in half, then put them in a sieve and rinse to remove all the syrup. Pat dry with kitchen paper and set aside.

Put the butter, sugar, eggs and ground almonds in a bowl. Sift in the flour and baking powder. Beat thoroughly until smooth, then stir in the cherries. Spoon the mixture into the prepared tin and smooth the top. Sprinkle the flaked almonds over the cake.

Bake in the preheated oven for 1½–1¾ hours, until well risen and a skewer inserted into the centre of the cake comes out clean.

Leave in the tin for 10 minutes, then turn out and place on a wire rack to cool.

# Gingerbread

serves 12–16

450 g/1 lb plain flour

1 tbsp baking powder

1 tsp bicarbonate of soda

1 tbsp ground ginger

175 g/6 oz unsalted butter, plus extra for greasing

175 g/6 oz soft dark brown sugar

175 g/6 oz black treacle

175 g/6 oz golden syrup

1 egg, beaten

300 ml/10 fl oz milk

Preheat the oven to 160°C/325°F/Gas Mark 3. Grease a 23-cm/9-inch square cake tin and line with baking paper.

Sift the flour, baking powder, bicarbonate of soda and ground ginger into a large mixing bowl.

Place the butter, sugar, treacle and golden syrup in a medium saucepan and heat over a low heat until the butter has melted and the sugar has dissolved. Allow to cool slightly.

Mix the egg with the milk and add to the cooled butter mixture.

Add all the liquid ingredients to the flour mixture and beat well using a wooden spoon until the mixture is smooth and glossy.

Pour the mixture into the prepared tin and bake in the centre of the preheated oven for 1½ hours, until well risen and just firm to the touch. This gives a lovely sticky gingerbread, but if you like a firmer cake cook for a further 15 minutes.

Remove from the oven and allow the cake to cool in the tin. When cool, remove the cake from the tin.

# Jewel-topped Madeira Cake

*serves 8–10*

225 g/8 oz butter, softened, plus extra for greasing

225 g/8 oz golden caster sugar

finely grated rind of 1 lemon

4 eggs, beaten

350 g/12 oz self-raising flour, sifted

2–3 tbsp milk

*fruit topping*

2½ tbsp honey

300 g/10½ oz glacé fruit, sliced

Preheat the oven to 160°C/325°F/Gas Mark 3. Grease a 20-cm/8-inch deep round cake tin and line with baking paper.

Put the butter, sugar and lemon rind in a bowl and beat together until light and fluffy. Gradually beat in the eggs. Gently fold in the flour, adding enough milk to give a soft dropping consistency.

Spoon the mixture into the prepared tin and bake in the preheated oven for 1½–1¾ hours, until risen and golden and a skewer inserted into the centre comes out clean.

Leave in the tin for 10 minutes, then turn out, remove the paper and place on a wire rack to cool. To make the topping, brush the honey over the cake and arrange the fruit on top.

# Honey Spice Cake

*serves 8–10*

150 g/5½ oz butter, plus extra for greasing

175 g/6 oz light muscovado sugar

250 g/9 oz honey

225 g/8 oz self-raising flour

½ tsp ground ginger

½ tsp ground cinnamon

½ tsp caraway seeds

seeds from 8 cardamom pods, ground

2 eggs, beaten

280 g/10 oz icing sugar

Preheat the oven to 180°C/350°F/Gas Mark 4. Grease a 23-cm/9-inch round cake tin and line with baking paper.

Put the butter, muscovado sugar, honey and 1 tablespoon of water into a saucepan. Heat gently until the butter has melted and the sugar has dissolved. Remove from the heat and leave to cool for 10 minutes.

Sift the flour into a bowl and mix in the ginger, cinnamon, caraway seeds and cardamom seeds. Make a well in the centre, pour in the honey mixture and the eggs, and beat well until smooth.

Pour the mixture into the prepared tin and bake in the preheated oven for 40–50 minutes, until well risen and a skewer inserted into the centre comes out clean. Leave in the tin for 5 minutes, then transfer to a wire rack to cool.

To make the icing, sift the icing sugar into a bowl. Stir in enough warm water to make a smooth flowing icing. Spoon over the cake, letting it flow down the sides. Leave to set before serving.

# Apple Upside-down Cake

*serves 6–8*

700 g/1 lb 9 oz cooking apples

8 cloves

250 g/9 oz caster sugar

140 g/5 oz butter, plus extra for greasing

2 eggs

25 g/1 oz flaked almonds, lightly toasted

25 g/1 oz hazelnuts, lightly toasted and ground

125 ml/4 fl oz double cream

125 ml/4 fl oz milk

½ tsp ground mixed spice

150 g/5½ oz self-raising flour, sifted

whipped cream, to serve

Preheat the oven to 180°C/350°F/Gas Mark 4. Grease a 20-cm/8-inch round cake tin.

Bring a large saucepan of water to the boil. Peel and core the apples, cut into slices, then add them to the pan with the cloves. Lower the heat and simmer for 5 minutes, then remove from the heat. Drain well. Discard the cloves. Leave the apples to cool a little.

Arrange the cooked apples slices over the bottom of the prepared tin and sprinkle over 2 tablespoons of the sugar.

In a separate bowl, cream together the butter and the remaining sugar. Gradually mix in the eggs, then the nuts, cream, milk and mixed spice. Gradually beat in the flour until smooth. Spread the mixture evenly over the apples, then bake the cake in the preheated oven for about 40 minutes, until golden and a skewer inserted into the centre comes out clean.

Remove from the oven and leave to cool in the tin for 5 minutes, then turn out onto a serving plate. Serve hot with whipped cream.

# Blueberry & Lemon Drizzle Cake

*serves 9*

225 g/8 oz butter, softened, plus extra for greasing

225 g/8 oz golden caster sugar

4 eggs, beaten

250 g/9 oz self-raising flour, sifted

finely grated rind of 1 lemon

25 g/1 oz ground almonds

juice of 1 lemon

200 g/7 oz fresh blueberries

*topping*

juice of 2 lemons

115 g/4 oz golden caster sugar

55 g/2 oz icing sugar

Preheat the oven to 180°C/350°F/Gas Mark 4. Grease a 20-cm/8-inch square cake tin and line with baking paper.

Put the butter and caster sugar in a bowl and beat together until light and fluffy. Gradually beat in the eggs, adding a little flour towards the end to prevent curdling. Beat in the lemon rind, then fold in the remaining flour and the almonds with enough lemon juice to give a dropping consistency.

Fold in three quarters of the blueberries and spoon into the prepared tin. Smooth the surface, then scatter the remaining blueberries on top. Bake in the preheated oven for about 1 hour, until firm to the touch and a skewer inserted into the centre comes out clean.

Meanwhile, make the topping. Put the lemon juice and caster sugar into a bowl and mix together. As soon as the cake comes out of the oven, prick it all over with a fine skewer and pour over the lemon mixture. Mix the icing sugar with a little water and drizzle over the cake. Leave in the tin until completely cold, then cut into squares.

# Banana & Lime Cake

serves 8–10

butter, for greasing

300 g/10½ oz plain flour

1 tsp salt

1½ tsp baking powder

175 g/6 oz soft light brown sugar

1 tsp grated lime rind

1 egg, lightly beaten

1 banana, mashed with 1 tbsp lime juice

150 ml/5 fl oz low-fat natural yogurt

115 g/4 oz sultanas

*topping*

125 g/4½ oz icing sugar

1–2 tsp lime juice

½ tsp finely grated lime rind

Preheat the oven to 180°C/350°F/Gas Mark 4. Grease an 18-cm/7-inch deep round cake tin and line with baking paper.

Sift the flour, salt and baking powder into a mixing bowl and stir in the brown sugar and lime rind.

Make a well in the centre of the dry ingredients and add the egg, banana, yogurt and sultanas. Mix well until thoroughly incorporated.

Spoon the mixture into the prepared tin and smooth the surface. Bake in the preheated oven for 40–45 minutes, until firm to the touch and a skewer inserted into the centre comes out clean. Leave to cool in the tin for 10 minutes, then turn out onto a wire rack.

To make the topping, sift the icing sugar into a small bowl and mix with the lime juice to form a soft but not too runny icing. Stir in the grated lime rind. Drizzle the lime icing over the cake, letting it run down the sides. Leave to set for 15 minutes.

# Marble Cake

*serves 10*

55 g/2 oz plain chocolate

1 tbsp strong black coffee

280 g/10 oz self-raising flour

1 tsp baking powder

225 g/8 oz butter, softened, plus extra for greasing

225 g/8 oz golden caster sugar

4 eggs, beaten

50 g/1¾ oz ground almonds

2 tbsp milk

1 tsp vanilla extract

*icing*

125 g/4½ oz plain chocolate

2 tbsp butter

Preheat the oven to 180°C/350°F/Gas Mark 4. Grease a 1.7-litre/3-pint ring mould.

Put the chocolate and coffee in a heatproof bowl set over a saucepan of gently simmering water. Heat until melted. Leave to cool.

Sift the flour and baking powder into a bowl. Add the butter, sugar, eggs, ground almonds and milk. Beat well until smooth.

Transfer half of the mixture to a separate bowl and stir in the vanilla extract. Stir the cooled chocolate mixture into the other half of the mixture. Place spoonfuls of the two mixtures alternately into the prepared ring mould, then drag a skewer through to create a marbled effect. Smooth the top.

Bake in the preheated oven for 50–60 minutes, until risen and a skewer inserted into the centre comes out clean. Leave in the mould for 5 minutes, then turn out onto a wire rack to cool.

To make the icing, put the chocolate, butter and 2 tablespoons of water into a heatproof bowl set over a saucepan of gently simmering water. Heat until melted. Stir and pour over the cake, working quickly to coat the top and sides. Leave to set before serving.

# Chocolate Lamington Cake

*serves 6*

175 g/6 oz butter or margarine, plus extra for greasing

175 g/6 oz caster sugar

3 eggs, lightly beaten

175 g/6 oz self-raising flour

2 tbsp cocoa powder

50 g/1¾ oz plain chocolate, broken into pieces

5 tbsp milk

1 tsp butter

85 g/3 oz icing sugar

about 8 tbsp desiccated coconut

150 ml/5 fl oz double cream, whipped

Preheat the oven to 180°C/350°F/Gas Mark 4. Grease a 450-g/1-lb loaf tin and line with baking paper.

Cream together the butter and sugar in a bowl until light and fluffy. Gradually add the eggs, beating well after each addition. Sift the flour and cocoa together. Fold into the mixture.

Pour the mixture into the prepared tin and smooth the surface. Bake in the preheated oven for 40 minutes, or until springy to the touch. Leave to cool for 5 minutes in the tin, then turn out onto a wire rack to cool completely.

Place the chocolate, milk and butter in a heatproof bowl set over a saucepan of gently simmering water. Stir until the chocolate has melted. Add the icing sugar and beat until smooth. Leave the icing to cool until it is thick enough to spread, then spread it all over the cake. Sprinkle with the desiccated coconut and leave to stand until the icing has set.

Cut a V-shaped wedge from the top of the cake. Put the cream in a piping bag fitted with a plain or star nozzle. Pipe the cream down the centre of the channel, then replace the wedge of cake. Pipe cream down either side of the wedge of cake.

# Pear & Ginger Cake

*serves 8–10*

200 g/7 oz unsalted butter, softened, plus extra for greasing

200 g/7 oz caster sugar

200 g/7 oz self-raising flour, sifted

1 tbsp ground ginger

3 eggs, lightly beaten

450 g/1 lb dessert pears, peeled, cored and thinly sliced

1 tbsp soft light brown sugar

Preheat the oven to 180°C/350°F/Gas Mark 4. Grease a 20-cm/8-inch deep round cake tin and line with baking paper.

Put 175 g/6 oz of the butter and the caster sugar into a bowl. Sift in the flour and ground ginger and add the eggs. Beat well with a whisk to form a smooth consistency.

Spoon the mixture into the prepared tin, smoothing the surface with a palette knife. Arrange the pear slices over the cake mixture. Sprinkle with the brown sugar and dot with the remaining butter.

Bake in the preheated oven for 35–40 minutes, or until the cake is golden and feels springy to the touch.

Leave the cake to cool slightly in the tin, then turn out onto a wire rack to cool completely.

# Honey & Almond Cake

*serves 8*

75 g/2¾ oz soft margarine, plus extra for greasing

75 g/2¾ oz soft light brown sugar

2 eggs

175 g/6 oz self-raising flour

1 tsp baking powder

4 tbsp milk

2 tbsp clear honey

50 g/1¾ oz flaked almonds

*syrup*

225 g/8 oz honey

2 tbsp lemon juice

Preheat the oven to 180°C/350°F/Gas Mark 4. Grease an 18-cm/7-inch round cake tin and line with baking paper.

Place the margarine, sugar, eggs, flour, baking powder, milk and honey in a large mixing bowl and beat well with a wooden spoon for about 1 minute, or until all of the ingredients are thoroughly mixed together.

Spoon into the prepared tin, smooth the surface with the back of a spoon or a knife and sprinkle with the almonds.

Bake in the preheated oven for about 50 minutes, or until well risen and a skewer inserted into the centre comes out clean.

Meanwhile, make the syrup. Combine the honey and lemon juice in a small saucepan and simmer over a low heat for about 5 minutes, or until the syrup coats the back of a spoon.

As soon as the cake comes out of the oven, pour the syrup over it, letting it soak into the cake.

Leave the cake to cool in the tin for at least 2 hours before slicing.

# Coconut Cake

*serves 6–8*

225 g/8 oz self-raising flour

pinch of salt

115 g/4 oz butter, cut into small pieces, plus extra for greasing

115 g/4 oz demerara sugar

100 g/3½ oz grated coconut, plus extra for sprinkling

2 eggs, lightly beaten

4 tbsp milk

Preheat the oven to 160°C/325°F/Gas Mark 3. Grease a 900-g/2-lb loaf tin and line with baking paper.

Sift the flour and salt into a mixing bowl and rub in the butter with your fingertips until the mixture resembles fine breadcrumbs.

Stir in the sugar, coconut, eggs and milk and mix to a soft dropping consistency.

Spoon the mixture into the prepared tin and smooth the surface with a palette knife. Bake in the preheated oven for 30 minutes.

Remove the cake from the oven and sprinkle with the extra coconut. Return the cake to the oven and bake for an additional 30 minutes, until well risen and golden and a skewer inserted into the centre comes out clean.

Leave the cake to cool slightly in the tin, then turn out onto a wire rack to cool completely.

# Banana & Cranberry Loaf

*serves 8–10*

butter, for greasing

175 g/6 oz self-raising flour

½ tsp baking powder

150 g/5½ oz soft light brown sugar

2 bananas, mashed

50 g/1¾ oz chopped mixed peel

25 g/1 oz chopped mixed nuts

50 g/1¾ oz dried cranberries

5–6 tbsp orange juice

2 eggs, beaten

150 ml/5 fl oz sunflower oil

75 g/2¾ oz icing sugar, sifted

grated rind of 1 orange

Preheat the oven to 180°C/350°F/Gas Mark 4. Grease a 900-g/2-lb loaf tin and line with baking paper.

Sift the flour and baking powder into a mixing bowl. Stir in the sugar, bananas, mixed peel, nuts and cranberries.

Mix the orange juice, eggs and oil together in a separate bowl until well combined. Add to the dry ingredients and mix until well blended. Pour the mixture into the prepared tin.

Bake in the preheated oven for about 1 hour, until firm to the touch and a skewer inserted into the centre comes out clean. Turn out onto a wire rack to cool.

Mix the icing sugar with a little water and drizzle the icing over the loaf. Sprinkle over the orange rind and leave the icing to set before serving.

# Slices &
# Bars

# Pecan Brownies

*makes 20*

70 g/2½ oz plain chocolate

140 g/5 oz plain flour

¾ tsp bicarbonate of soda

¼ tsp baking powder

225 g/8 oz unsalted butter, plus extra for greasing

100 g/3½ oz demerara sugar, plus extra for sprinkling

½ tsp almond extract

1 egg

55 g/2 oz pecan nuts

1 tsp milk

icing sugar, for dusting

Preheat the oven to 180°C/350°F/Gas Mark 4. Grease a large baking sheet and line with baking paper.

Put the chocolate in a heatproof bowl set over a saucepan of gently simmering water and heat until melted. Meanwhile, sift together the flour, bicarbonate of soda and baking powder into a large bowl.

In a separate bowl, cream together the butter and sugar, then mix in the almond extract and egg. Remove the chocolate from the heat and stir into the butter mixture. Chop the pecan nuts finely, then add them to the bowl, along with the flour mixture and milk, and stir until well combined.

Spoon the mixture onto the prepared baking sheet and smooth the surface. Transfer to the preheated oven and bake for 30 minutes, or until firm to the touch (it should still be a little gooey in the middle). Remove from the oven and leave to cool completely. Remove from the baking sheet and cut into 20 squares. Sprinkle with sugar and serve.

# Maple-glazed Pistachio Brownies

*makes 16*

175 g/6 oz unsalted butter,
plus extra for greasing

115 g/4 oz plain chocolate

250 g/9 oz caster sugar

4 eggs, beaten

1 tsp vanilla extract

200 g/7 oz plain flour

85 g/3 oz pistachio nuts,
chopped

*glaze*

115 g/4 oz plain chocolate

115 g/4 oz crème fraîche

2 tbsp maple syrup

Preheat the oven to 190°C/375°F/Gas Mark 5. Lightly grease a 30 x 20-cm/12 x 8-inch shallow rectangular baking tin.

Place the butter and chocolate in a small pan over a very low heat and stir until melted. Remove from the heat. Whisk the sugar, eggs and vanilla extract together in a large bowl until pale. Beat in the melted chocolate mixture. Fold in the flour evenly, then stir in 55 g/2 oz of the pistachio nuts.

Spoon into the prepared tin and smooth the surface. Bake in the preheated oven for 25–30 minutes, or until firm and golden brown.

For the glaze, melt the chocolate in a heatproof bowl set over a pan of gently simmering water. Stir in the crème fraîche and maple syrup and beat until smooth and glossy.

Spread the glaze evenly over the brownies with a palette knife. Sprinkle with the remaining pistachio nuts and leave until the topping is set.

# White Chocolate Chip Brownies

*makes 8*

115 g/4 oz butter, plus extra for greasing

225 g/8 oz white chocolate, roughly chopped

2 eggs

115 g/4 oz soft light brown sugar

115 g/4 oz self-raising flour

75 g/2¾ oz walnut pieces, roughly chopped

Preheat the oven to 180°C/350°F/Gas Mark 4. Grease an 18-cm/7-inch square cake tin and line with baking paper.

Put the butter and 175 g/6 oz of the chocolate in a heatproof bowl set over a saucepan of gently simmering water. When melted, stir together, then set aside to cool slightly.

Whisk the eggs and sugar together, then beat in the cooled chocolate mixture until well mixed. Fold in the flour, the remaining chocolate and the walnuts. Pour the mixture into the prepared tin and smooth the surface.

Transfer the tin to the preheated oven and bake for about 30 minutes, until just set. The mixture should still be a little soft in the centre. Leave to cool in the tin, then cut into rectangles before serving.

# Apricot Blondies

*makes 12*

350 g/12 oz white chocolate

85 g/3 oz unsalted butter, plus extra for greasing

1 tsp vanilla extract

3 eggs, beaten

140 g/5½ oz light muscovado sugar

115 g/4 oz self-raising flour

85 g/3 oz macadamia nuts, roughly chopped

100 g/3½ oz ready-to-eat dried apricots, roughly chopped

Preheat the oven to 190°C/375°F/Gas Mark 5. Grease a 28 x 18-cm/11 x 7-inch rectangular baking tin and line with baking paper.

Chop half the chocolate into small chunks. Melt the remaining chocolate with the butter in a small pan over a very low heat and stir until melted. Remove from the heat and stir in the vanilla extract.

Whisk the eggs and sugar together in a large bowl until pale. Beat in the melted chocolate mixture. Fold in the flour evenly, then stir in the macadamia nuts, apricots and chopped chocolate.

Spoon into the prepared tin and smooth the surface. Bake in the preheated oven for 25–30 minutes, or until firm and golden brown.

Leave to cool in the tin. Turn out when cold and cut into triangles.

# Upside-down Toffee Apple Squares

*makes 9*

*toffee apple topping*

85 g/3 oz light muscovado sugar

55 g/2 oz unsalted butter

1 dessert apple, cored and thinly sliced

115 g/4 oz unsalted butter, plus extra for greasing

115 g/6 oz light muscovado sugar

2 eggs, beaten

200 g/7 oz plain flour

1 tsp baking powder

½ tsp bicarbonate of soda

1½ tsp ground mixed spice

2 eating apples, peeled and coarsely grated

85 g/3 oz hazelnuts, chopped

Preheat the oven to 180°C/350°F/Gas Mark 4. Grease a 23-cm/9-inch shallow square cake tin.

For the topping, place the sugar and butter in a small pan and heat gently, stirring, until melted. Pour into the prepared tin. Arrange the apple slices over the mixture.

Place the butter and sugar in a bowl and beat well until pale and fluffy. Beat in the eggs gradually.

Sift together the flour, baking powder, bicarbonate of soda and mixed spice, and fold into the mixture. Stir in the grated apples and hazelnuts.

Pour into the prepared tin and bake in the preheated oven for 35–40 minutes, until firm and golden. Cool in the tin for 10 minutes, then turn out and cut into squares.

# Carrot Streusel Bars

*makes 15*

115 g/4 oz unsalted butter, softened, plus extra for greasing

350 g/12 oz light muscovado sugar

2 eggs, beaten

1 tsp vanilla extract

175 g/6 oz plain flour

½ tsp bicarbonate of soda

½ tsp baking powder

85 g/3 oz sultanas

125 g/4½ oz carrots, finely grated

55 g/2 oz chopped walnuts

*streusel topping*

40 g/1½ oz finely chopped walnuts

40 g/1½ oz dark muscovado sugar

15 g/½ oz plain flour

½ tsp ground cinnamon

15 g/½ oz unsalted butter, melted

Preheat the oven to 180°C/350°F/Gas Mark 4. Grease a 30 x 20-cm/12 x 8-inch shallow rectangular baking tin and line with baking paper.

Cream together the butter and sugar until pale. Beat in the eggs and vanilla extract. Sift the flour, bicarbonate of soda and baking powder into the mixture and fold in evenly. Stir in the sultanas, carrots and walnuts.

Spoon the mixture into the prepared tin. Mix together all the topping ingredients to make a crumbly mixture and sprinkle evenly over the cake mixture.

Bake in the preheated oven for 45–55 minutes, or until golden brown and just firm to the touch. Cool in the tin, then cut into bars.

# Gingerbread Squares

*makes 24*

90 g/3¼ oz butter or
margarine, plus extra
for greasing

55 g/2 oz dark muscovado
sugar

5 tbsp black treacle

1 egg white

1 tsp almond extract

175 g/6 oz plain flour, plus
extra for dusting

¼ tsp bicarbonate of soda

¼ tsp baking powder

pinch of salt

½ tsp mixed spice

½ tsp ground ginger

125 g/4½ oz dessert apples,
cooked and
finely chopped

Preheat the oven to 180°C/350°F/Gas Mark 4. Grease a large baking sheet and line with baking paper. Put the butter, sugar, treacle, egg white and almond extract into a food processor and blend until smooth.

In a separate bowl, sift the flour, bicarbonate of soda, baking powder, salt, mixed spice and ginger together. Add to the creamed mixture and beat together thoroughly. Stir in the chopped apples. Pour the mixture onto the prepared baking sheet.

Transfer to the preheated oven and bake for 10 minutes, or until golden brown. Remove from the oven and cut into 24 pieces. Transfer to a wire rack to cool completely before serving.

# Almond Slices

*makes 8*

60 g/2¼ oz ground almonds

140 g/5 oz dried milk powder

200 g/7 oz granulated sugar

½ tsp saffron threads

115 g/4 oz unsalted butter, plus extra for greasing

3 eggs, lightly beaten

1 tbsp flaked almonds

Preheat the oven to 160°C/325°F/Gas Mark 3. Grease a 20-cm/8-inch shallow square cake tin and line with baking paper.

Place the ground almonds, milk powder, sugar and saffron in a large mixing bowl and stir to mix well.

Melt the butter in a small saucepan over a low heat. Pour the melted butter over the dry ingredients and mix well with a wooden spoon until thoroughly combined. Add the beaten eggs to the mixture and stir to blend well.

Spread the mixture evenly in the prepared tin, sprinkle with the flaked almonds and bake in the preheated oven for 45 minutes, or until a skewer inserted into the centre comes out clean.

Remove from the oven and cut into triangles.

# Chocolate Chip & Walnut Slices

*makes* 18

115 g/4 oz walnut pieces

225 g/8 oz butter, plus extra for greasing

175 g/6 oz caster sugar

few drops of vanilla extract

225 g/8 oz plain flour

200 g/7 oz plain chocolate chips

Preheat the oven to 180°C/350°F/Gas Mark 4. Grease a 20 x 30-cm/8 x 12-inch Swiss roll tin and line with baking paper.

Coarsely chop the walnut pieces to about the same size as the chocolate chips and set aside.

Beat the butter and sugar together until pale and fluffy. Add the vanilla extract, then stir in the flour. Stir in the reserved walnuts and the chocolate chips. Press the mixture into the prepared tin.

Bake in the preheated oven for 20–25 minutes, until golden brown. Leave to cool in the tin, then cut into slices.

# Strawberry & Chocolate Slices

*makes 16*

225 g/8 oz plain flour

1 tsp baking powder

100 g/3½ oz caster sugar

85 g/3 oz soft light brown sugar

225 g/8 oz unsalted butter, plus extra for greasing

150 g/5½ oz rolled oats

225 g/8 oz strawberry jam

100 g/3½ oz plain chocolate chips

25 g/1 oz flaked almonds

Preheat the oven to 190°C/375°F/Gas Mark 5. Grease a 30 x 20-cm/12 x 8-inch deep rectangular baking tin and line with baking paper.

Sift the flour and baking powder into a large bowl. Add the caster sugar and brown sugar and mix well. Add the butter and rub in with your fingertips until the mixture resembles breadcrumbs. Stir in the oats.

Press three quarters of the mixture into the base of the prepared tin. Bake in the preheated oven for 10 minutes.

Spread the jam over the cooked base, then sprinkle over the chocolate chips. Mix the remaining flour mixture with the almonds. Sprinkle evenly over the chocolate chips and press down gently.

Return to the oven and bake for a further 20–25 minutes, until golden brown. Remove from the oven, leave to cool in the tin, then cut into slices.

# Hazelnut Squares

*makes 16*

150 g/5½ oz plain flour

pinch of salt

1 tsp baking powder

75 g/2¾ oz butter, cut into small pieces, plus extra for greasing

150 g/5½ oz soft light brown sugar

1 egg, lightly beaten

4 tbsp milk

150 g/5½ oz hazelnuts, halved

demerara sugar, for sprinkling (optional)

Preheat the oven to 180°C/350°F/Gas Mark 4. Grease a 23-cm/9-inch square cake tin and line with baking paper.

Sift the flour, salt and baking powder into a large bowl. Rub in the butter with your fingertips until the mixture resembles fine breadcrumbs. Stir in the brown sugar.

Add the egg, milk and hazelnuts to the mixture and stir well until thoroughly combined.

Spoon the mixture into the prepared cake tin, spreading it out evenly, and smooth the surface. Sprinkle with demerara sugar, if using.

Bake in the preheated oven for about 25 minutes, or until the mixture is firm to the touch.

Leave to cool for 10 minutes in the tin, then loosen the edges with a round-bladed knife and turn out onto a wire rack. Cut into squares and leave to cool completely before serving.

# Hazelnut Chocolate Crunch

*makes 12*

200 g/7 oz rolled oats

55 g/2 oz hazelnuts, lightly toasted and chopped

55 g/2 oz plain flour

115 g/4 oz unsalted butter, plus extra for greasing

85 g/3 oz light muscovado sugar

2 tbsp golden syrup

55 g/2 oz plain chocolate chips

Preheat the oven to 180°C/350°F/Gas Mark 4. Grease a 23-cm/9-inch shallow square cake tin.

Mix the oats, hazelnuts and flour in a large bowl.

Place the butter, sugar and golden syrup in a large saucepan and heat gently until the sugar has dissolved. Pour in the dry ingredients and mix well. Stir in the chocolate chips.

Turn the mixture into the prepared tin and bake in the preheated oven for 20–25 minutes, or until golden brown and firm to the touch.

Using a knife, mark into 12 triangles and leave to cool in the tin. Cut the triangles with a sharp knife before carefully removing them from the tin.

# Fruity Flapjacks

*makes 14*

140 g/5 oz rolled oats

115 g/4 oz demerara sugar

85 g/3 oz raisins

115 g/4 oz butter, melted, plus extra for greasing

Preheat the oven to 190°C/375°F/Gas Mark 5. Grease a 28 x 18-cm/11 x 7-inch shallow rectangular baking tin.

Combine the oats, sugar and raisins with the butter, stirring well. Spoon the mixture into the prepared tin and press down firmly with the back of a spoon. Bake in the preheated oven for 15–20 minutes, or until golden.

Using a sharp knife, mark into 14 bars, then leave to cool in the tin for 10 minutes. Carefully transfer the bars to a wire rack to cool completely.

# Apricot Flapjacks

*makes 10*

175 g/6 oz margarine, plus extra for greasing

85 g/3 oz demerara sugar

55 g/2 oz clear honey

140 g/5 oz dried apricots, chopped

2 tsp sesame seeds

225 g/8 oz rolled oats

Preheat the oven to 180°C/350°F/Gas Mark 4. Grease a 26 x 17-cm/10½ x 6½-inch shallow rectangular baking tin.

Put the margarine, sugar and honey into a small saucepan over a low heat and heat until the ingredients have melted together – do not boil. When the ingredients are well combined, stir in the apricots, sesame seeds and oats.

Spoon the mixture into the prepared tin and smooth the surface with the back of a spoon. Cook in the preheated oven for 20–25 minutes, or until golden brown.

Remove from the oven, cut into bars and leave to cool completely before removing from the tin.

# Chocolate Coconut Squares

*makes 9*

225 g/8 oz plain chocolate digestive biscuits

75 g/2¾ oz butter or margarine, plus extra for greasing

200 ml/7 fl oz canned evaporated milk

1 egg, beaten

1 tsp vanilla extract

2 tbsp caster sugar

40 g/1½ oz self-raising flour, sifted

125 g/4½ oz grated coconut

50 g/1¾ oz plain chocolate, melted

Preheat the oven to 190°C/375°F/Gas Mark 5. Grease a 20-cm/8-inch shallow square cake tin and line with baking paper.

Place the biscuits in a polythene bag and crush with a rolling pin or process them in a food processor.

Melt the butter in a saucepan and stir in the crushed biscuits thoroughly. Press the mixture into the base of the prepared tin.

Beat together the evaporated milk, egg, vanilla extract and sugar until smooth. Stir in the flour and grated coconut. Pour over the biscuit layer and use a palette knife to smooth the surface.

Bake in the preheated oven for 30 minutes, or until the coconut topping has become firm and just golden.

Leave to cool in the cake tin for about 5 minutes, then cut into squares. Leave to cool completely in the tin.

Carefully remove the squares from the tin and place them on a cutting board. Drizzle the melted chocolate over the squares and leave to set before serving.

# Ginger-topped Fingers

*makes 16*

225 g/8 oz plain flour

1 tsp ground ginger

85 g/3 oz golden caster sugar

175 g/6 oz butter, plus extra for greasing

*topping*

1 tbsp golden syrup

55 g/2 oz butter

4 tbsp icing sugar

1 tsp ground ginger

Preheat the oven to 180°C/350°F/Gas. Mark 4. Grease a 28 x 18-cm/11 x 7-inch rectangular baking tin.

Sift the flour and ginger into a bowl and stir in the sugar. Rub in the butter with your fingertips until the mixture begins to stick together.

Press the mixture into the prepared tin and smooth the surface with a palette knife. Bake in the preheated oven for 40 minutes, or until very lightly browned.

To make the topping, place the golden syrup and butter in a small saucepan over a low heat and stir until melted. Stir in 2 tablespoons of the icing sugar and the ginger. Remove the shortbread base from the oven and pour the topping over it while both are still hot.

Place the remaining icing sugar in a small bowl and stir in just enough water to form a thin icing. Spoon into a small piping bag fitted with a small plain nozzle and pipe horizontal lines over the ginger topping. Use a cocktail stick to pull vertical lines through the icing to create a feathered effect.

Leave to cool slightly in the tin, then cut into slices. Transfer to a wire rack to cool completely.

# Macadamia Nut Caramel Squares

*makes 16*

280 g/10 oz plain flour

175 g/6 oz soft light brown sugar

115 g/4 oz butter, plus extra for greasing

115 g/4 oz macadamia nuts, roughly chopped

*topping*

115 g/4 oz butter

100 g/3½ oz soft light brown sugar

200 g/7 oz milk chocolate chips

Preheat the oven to 180°C/350°F/Gas Mark 4. Grease a 30 x 20-cm/12 x 8-inch rectangular baking tin.

To make the base, sift the flour into a bowl and stir in the sugar. Rub in the butter with your fingertips until the mixture resembles fine breadcrumbs.

Press the mixture into the base of the prepared tin. Sprinkle over the macadamia nuts.

To make the topping, put the butter and sugar in a saucepan and slowly bring the mixture to the boil, stirring constantly. Boil for 1 minute, stirring constantly, then carefully pour the mixture over the macadamia nuts.

Bake in the preheated oven for about 20 minutes, until the caramel topping is bubbling. Remove from the oven and immediately sprinkle the chocolate chips evenly on top. Leave for 2–3 minutes, until the chocolate chips start to melt, then, using the blade of a knife, swirl the chocolate over the top. Leave to cool in the tin, then cut into squares.

# Cookies & Small Cakes

# White Chocolate Cookies

*makes 24*

115 g/4 oz butter, softened, plus extra for greasing

115 g/4 oz soft light brown sugar

1 egg, beaten

250 g/9 oz self-raising flour

pinch of salt

125 g/4½ oz white chocolate, chopped

50 g/1¾ oz Brazil nuts, chopped

Preheat the oven to 190°C/375°F/Gas Mark 5. Grease several baking sheets.

In a large mixing bowl, cream together the butter and sugar until light and fluffy.

Gradually add the egg to the creamed mixture, beating well after each addition.

Sift the flour and salt into the creamed mixture and blend well. Stir in the chocolate and Brazil nuts.

Place heaped teaspoonfuls of the mixture on the prepared baking sheets, spacing well to allow for spreading during cooking. Bake in the preheated oven for 10–12 minutes, or until just golden brown.

Transfer the cookies to wire racks and leave until completely cold.

# Sticky Ginger Cookies

*makes 20*

225 g/8 oz butter, softened,
plus extra for greasing

140 g/5 oz golden caster
sugar

1 egg yolk, lightly beaten

55 g/2 oz stem ginger,
roughly chopped, plus
1 tbsp syrup from the jar

280 g/10 oz plain flour

pinch of salt

55 g/2 oz plain chocolate
chips

Put the butter and sugar into a bowl and mix well with a wooden spoon, then beat in the egg yolk and ginger syrup.

Sift together the flour and salt into the mixture, add the stem ginger and chocolate chips and stir until thoroughly combined. Shape the mixture into a log, wrap in clingfilm and chill in the refrigerator for 30–60 minutes.

Preheat the oven to 190°C/375°F/Gas Mark 5. Grease two baking sheets and line with baking paper.

Unwrap the log and cut it into 5-mm/¼-inch slices with a sharp serrated knife. Put them onto the prepared baking sheets, spaced well apart.

Bake in the preheated oven for 12–15 minutes, until golden brown. Leave to cool on the baking sheets for 5–10 minutes, then, using a palette knife, carefully transfer the cookies to wire racks to cool completely.

# Chewy Golden Cookies

*makes 30*

175 g/6 oz butter or margarine, plus extra for greasing

250 g/9 oz soft light brown sugar

350 g/12 oz golden syrup

3 egg whites

250 g/9 oz rolled oats

280 g/10 oz plain flour

pinch of salt

1 tsp baking powder

2 tbsp icing sugar

Preheat the oven to 180°C/350°F/Gas Mark 4. Grease a large baking sheet and line with baking paper.

In a large mixing bowl, blend the butter, sugar, golden syrup and egg whites together. Gradually add the oats, flour, salt and baking powder and mix thoroughly.

Drop 30 rounded tablespoonfuls of the mixture onto the prepared baking sheet and transfer to the preheated oven. Bake for 12 minutes, or until the biscuits are light brown.

Remove from the oven and transfer to a wire rack to cool. Mix the icing sugar with a few drops of water to form a thin icing, drizzle over the biscuits and leave to set.

# Oaty Raisin & Hazelnut Cookies

*makes 30*

55 g/2 oz raisins, chopped

125 ml/4 fl oz orange juice

225 g/8 oz butter, softened, plus extra for greasing

140 g/5 oz caster sugar

1 egg yolk, lightly beaten

2 tsp vanilla extract

225 g/8 oz plain flour

pinch of salt

55 g/2 oz rolled oats

55 g/2 oz hazelnuts, chopped

whole hazelnuts, to decorate

Preheat the oven to 190°C/375°F/Gas Mark 5. Grease two baking sheets and line with baking paper.

Put the raisins in a bowl, add the orange juice and leave to soak for 10 minutes.

Put the butter and sugar into a bowl and mix well with a wooden spoon, then beat in the egg yolk and vanilla extract.

Sift together the flour and salt into the mixture and add the oats and chopped hazelnuts. Drain the raisins, add them to the mixture and stir until thoroughly combined.

Scoop up tablespoons of the mixture and place them in mounds on the prepared baking sheets, spaced well apart. Flatten slightly and place a whole hazelnut in the centre of each cookie.

Bake in the preheated oven for 12–15 minutes, until golden brown. Leave to cool on the baking sheets for 5–10 minutes, then, using a palette knife, carefully transfer the cookies to wire racks to cool completely.

# Almond & Raspberry Jam Drops

*makes 25*

225 g/8 oz butter, softened,
plus extra for greasing

140 g/5 oz caster sugar

1 egg yolk, lightly beaten

2 tsp almond extract

280 g/10 oz plain flour

pinch of salt

55 g/2 oz almonds, toasted
and chopped

55 g/2 oz chopped mixed
peel

4 tbsp raspberry jam

Preheat the oven to 190°C/375°F/Gas Mark 5. Grease two baking sheets and line with baking paper.

Put the butter and sugar into a bowl and mix well with a wooden spoon, then beat in the egg yolk and almond extract. Sift together the flour and salt into the mixture, add the almonds and mixed peel and stir until thoroughly combined.

Scoop up tablespoons of the mixture and shape into balls with your hands, then put them onto the prepared baking sheets, spaced well apart. Use the dampened handle of a wooden spoon to make a hollow in the centre of each cookie and fill the hollows with raspberry jam.

Bake in the preheated oven for 12–15 minutes, until golden brown. Leave to cool on the baking sheets for 5–10 minutes, then, using a palette knife, carefully transfer the cookies to wire racks to cool completely.

# Lemon Jumbles

*makes 50*

75 g/2¾ oz butter, softened, plus extra for greasing

115 g/4 oz caster sugar

grated rind of 1 lemon

1 egg, lightly beaten

4 tbsp lemon juice

350 g/12 oz plain flour, plus extra for dusting

1 tsp baking powder

1 tbsp milk

icing sugar, for dusting

Preheat the oven to 160°C/325°F/Gas Mark 3. Grease several baking sheets and line with baking paper.

In a mixing bowl, cream together the butter, caster sugar and lemon rind, until pale and fluffy.

Add the egg and lemon juice, a little at a time, beating well after each addition.

Sift the flour and baking powder into the creamed mixture and blend together. Add the milk, mixing to form a firm dough.

Turn the dough out on to a lightly floured work surface and divide into about 50 equal-sized pieces. Roll each piece into a sausage shape with your hands and twist in the middle to make an 'S' shape.

Place the biscuits on the prepared baking sheets and bake in the preheated oven for 15–20 minutes. Transfer to a wire rack and leave to cool completely. Dust generously with icing sugar before serving.

# Mocha Walnut Cookies

*makes 16*

115 g/4 oz butter, softened, plus extra for greasing

115 g/4 oz light muscovado sugar

85 g/3 oz caster sugar

1 tsp vanilla extract

1 tbsp instant coffee granules, dissolved in 1 tbsp hot water

1 egg

175 g/6 oz plain flour

½ tsp baking powder

¼ tsp bicarbonate of soda

55 g/2 oz milk chocolate chips

55 g/2 oz walnuts, roughly chopped

Preheat the oven to 180°C/350°F/Gas Mark 4. Grease two baking sheets and line with baking paper.

Put the butter, muscovado sugar and caster sugar in a bowl and beat until light and fluffy. Put the vanilla extract, coffee and egg in a separate bowl and whisk together.

Gradually add the coffee mixture to the butter and sugar mixture, beating until fluffy. Sift the flour, baking powder and bicarbonate of soda into the mixture and fold in carefully. Fold in the chocolate chips and walnuts.

Spoon heaped teaspoonfuls of the mixture onto the prepared baking sheets, allowing room for the cookies to spread. Bake in the preheated oven for 10–15 minutes, until crisp on the outside but still soft inside. Leave to cool on the baking sheets for 2 minutes, then transfer to wire racks to cool completely.

# Chocolate Sprinkle Cookies

*makes 30*

225 g/8 oz butter, softened, plus extra for greasing

140 g/5 oz caster sugar

1 egg yolk, lightly beaten

2 tsp vanilla extract

225 g/8 oz plain flour, plus extra for dusting

55 g/2 oz cocoa powder

pinch of salt

200 g/7 oz white chocolate, broken into pieces

85 g/3 oz chocolate vermicelli

Put the butter and sugar into a bowl and mix well with a wooden spoon, then beat in the egg yolk and vanilla extract. Sift together the flour, cocoa powder and salt into the mixture and stir until thoroughly combined. Halve the dough, roll each piece into a ball, wrap in clingfilm and chill in the refrigerator for 30–60 minutes to firm up.

Preheat the oven to 190°C/375°F/Gas Mark 5. Grease two baking sheets and line with baking paper.

Unwrap the dough and roll out between 2 pieces of baking parchment to about 5 mm/¼ inch thick and stamp out 30 cookies with a 6–7-cm/2½–2¾-inch fluted round cutter. Put them on the prepared baking sheets, spaced well apart.

Bake in the preheated oven for 10–12 minutes. Leave to cool on the baking sheets for 5–10 minutes, then, using a palette knife, carefully transfer the cookies to wire racks to cool completely.

Put the white chocolate into a heatproof bowl set over a pan of gently simmering water until melted, then immediately remove from the heat. Spread the melted chocolate over the cookies, leave to cool slightly, then sprinkle with the chocolate vermicelli. Leave to cool and set.

# Rum & Raisin Sandwich Cookies

*makes 15*

100 g/3½ oz raisins

150 ml/5 fl oz rum

225 g/8 oz butter, softened, plus extra for greasing

140 g/5 oz caster sugar

1 egg yolk, lightly beaten

280 g/10 oz plain flour

pinch of salt

*orange filling*

175 g/6 oz icing sugar

85 g/3 oz butter, softened

2 tsp finely grated orange rind

1 tsp rum

few drops of yellow food colouring (optional)

Put the raisins into a bowl, pour in the rum and leave to soak for 15 minutes, then drain, reserving any remaining rum.

Preheat the oven to 190°C/375°F/Gas Mark 5. Grease two baking sheets and line with baking paper.

Put the butter and sugar into a bowl and mix well with a wooden spoon, then beat in the egg yolk and 2 teaspoons of the reserved rum. Sift together the flour and salt into the mixture, add the raisins and stir until thoroughly combined.

Scoop up tablespoons of the dough and put them on the prepared baking sheets, spaced well apart. Flatten gently and smooth the tops with the tines of a fork.

Bake in the preheated oven for 10–15 minutes, until light golden brown. Leave to cool on the baking sheets for 5–10 minutes, then, using a palette knife, carefully transfer to wire racks to cool completely.

To make the orange filling, sift the icing sugar into a bowl, add the butter, orange rind, rum and food colouring, if using, and beat well until smooth. Spread the filling over half the cookies and top with the remaining cookies.

# Chocolate Chip Shortbread

*makes 8*

115 g/4 oz plain flour

55 g/2 oz cornflour

55 g/2 oz golden caster sugar

115 g/4 oz butter, diced, plus extra for greasing

40 g/1½ oz plain chocolate chips

Preheat the oven to 160°C/325°F/Gas Mark 3. Grease a 23-cm/9-inch loose-based fluted tart tin.

Sift the flour and cornflour into a large bowl. Stir in the sugar, then add the butter and rub it in with your fingertips until the mixture starts to bind together.

Turn into the prepared tart tin and press evenly over the base. Prick the surface with a fork. Sprinkle with the chocolate chips and press lightly into the surface.

Bake in the preheated oven for 35–40 minutes, or until cooked but not brown. Mark into 8 portions with a sharp knife. Leave to cool in the tin for 10 minutes, then transfer to a wire rack to cool completely.

# Viennese Chocolate Fingers

### makes 18

115 g/4 oz unsalted butter, plus extra for greasing

6 tbsp icing sugar

225 g/8 oz self-raising flour, sifted

3 tbsp cornflour

200 g/7 oz plain chocolate, broken into pieces

Preheat the oven to 190°C/375°F/Gas Mark 5. Grease two baking sheets and line with baking paper.

Beat the butter and sugar in a mixing bowl until light and fluffy. Gradually beat in the flour and cornflour.

Put 75 g/2¾ oz of the chocolate in a heatproof bowl set over a saucepan of gently simmering water and stir until melted. Beat the melted chocolate into the mixture.

Place in a piping bag fitted with a large star nozzle and pipe fingers about 5 cm/2 inches long onto the prepared baking sheets, allowing room for the biscuits to spread during cooking.

Bake in the preheated oven for 12–15 minutes. Leave to cool slightly on the baking sheets, then transfer to a wire rack and leave to cool completely.

Melt the remaining chocolate as above. Dip one end of each biscuit in the chocolate, allowing the excess to drip back into the bowl.

Place the biscuits on a sheet of baking paper and leave the chocolate to set before serving.

# Cherry & Sultana Scones

*makes 8*

225 g/8 oz self-raising flour, plus extra for dusting

1 tbsp caster sugar

pinch of salt

85 g/3 oz butter, cut into small pieces, plus extra for greasing

3 tbsp glacé cherries, chopped

3 tbsp sultanas

1 egg, lightly beaten

3 tbsp milk

Preheat the oven to 220°C/425°F/Gas Mark 7. Grease a baking sheet and line with baking paper.

Sift the flour, sugar and salt into a mixing bowl and rub in the butter with your fingertips until the mixture resembles breadcrumbs.

Stir in the glacé cherries and sultanas. Add the egg. Reserve 1 tablespoon of the milk for glazing, then add the remainder to the mixture. Mix well together to form a soft dough.

On a lightly floured work surface, roll out the dough to a thickness of 2 cm/¾ inch and cut out 8 circles using a 5-cm/2-inch round cutter.

Place the scones on the prepared baking sheet and brush the tops with the reserved milk.

Bake in the preheated oven for 8–10 minutes, or until the scones are golden brown. Transfer the scones to a wire rack to cool completely.

# Lemon Butterfly Cakes

*makes 12*

115 g/4 oz self-raising flour

½ tsp baking powder

115 g/4 oz butter, softened

115 g/4 oz caster sugar

2 eggs, beaten

finely grated rind of ¾ lemon

2–4 tbsp milk

icing sugar, for dusting

*filling*

55 g/2 oz butter

115 g/4 oz icing sugar

1 tbsp lemon juice

Preheat the oven to 190°C/375°F/Gas Mark 5. Place 12 paper cases in a bun tin.

Sift the flour and baking powder into a bowl. Add the butter, caster sugar, eggs, lemon rind and enough milk to give a medium-soft consistency. Beat the mixture thoroughly until smooth, then divide between the paper cases.

Bake in the preheated oven for 15–20 minutes, or until well risen and golden. Transfer to wire racks to cool.

To make the filling, place the butter in a bowl. Sift in the icing sugar and add the lemon juice. Beat well until smooth and creamy.

When the cakes are completely cooled, use a sharp-pointed vegetable knife to cut a circle from the top of each cake, then cut each circle in half.

Spoon a little buttercream on top of each cake and press the 2 semi-circular pieces into it to resemble wings. Dust the cakes with icing sugar before serving.

# Devil's Food Cakes with Chocolate Icing

*makes 18*

50 g/1¾ oz soft margarine

115 g/4 oz soft dark brown sugar

2 large eggs

115 g/4 oz plain flour

½ tsp bicarbonate of soda

25 g/1 oz cocoa powder

125 ml/4 fl oz soured cream

chocolate caraque, to decorate

*icing*

125 g/4½ oz plain chocolate, broken into pieces

2 tbsp caster sugar

150 ml/5 fl oz soured cream

Preheat the oven to 180°C/350°F/Gas Mark 4. Place 18 paper cases in a bun tin.

Put the margarine, brown sugar, eggs, flour, bicarbonate of soda and cocoa powder in a large bowl and, using an electric hand whisk, beat together until just smooth. Using a metal spoon, fold in the soured cream. Spoon the mixture into the paper cases.

Bake the cupcakes in the preheated oven for 20 minutes, or until well risen and firm to the touch. Transfer to a wire rack to cool.

To make the icing, put the chocolate into a heatproof bowl set over a saucepan of gently simmering water and heat until melted, stirring occasionally. Remove from the heat and allow to cool slightly, then whisk in the caster sugar and soured cream until combined. Spread the icing over the tops of the cupcakes and leave to set in the refrigerator before serving. Serve decorated with chocolate caraque.

# Chocolate Chip Cupcakes

*makes 18*

85 g/3 oz butter, softened

100 g/3½ oz caster sugar

2 eggs, lightly beaten

2 tbsp milk

55 g/2 oz plain chocolate chips

225 g/8 oz self-raising flour

25 g/1 oz cocoa powder, plus extra for dusting

*icing*

225 g/8 oz white chocolate, broken into pieces

150 g/5½ oz cream cheese

Preheat the oven to 200°C/400°F/Gas Mark 6. Place 18 paper cases in a bun tin.

Beat together the butter and sugar until pale and fluffy. Gradually add the eggs, beating well after each addition. Add a little of the flour if the mixture starts to curdle. Add the milk, then fold in the chocolate chips.

Sift together the flour and cocoa and fold into the mixture with a metal spoon or palette knife. Divide the batter equally between the paper cases and smooth the surfaces.

Bake in the preheated oven for 20 minutes, or until well risen and springy to the touch. Cool on a wire rack.

To make the icing, melt the chocolate in a heatproof bowl set over a saucepan of gently simmering water. Cool slightly. Beat the cream cheese until softened, then beat in the melted chocolate. Spread a little of the icing over each cake and leave to chill for 1 hour. Dust with a little cocoa before serving.

# Chocolate Chunk Muffins

*makes 12*

280 g/10 oz plain flour

1 tbsp baking powder

⅛ tsp salt

115 g/4 oz caster sugar

175 g/6 oz chocolate chunks

2 eggs

250 ml/9 fl oz milk

6 tbsp sunflower oil or 85 g/ 3 oz butter, melted and cooled

1 tsp vanilla extract

Preheat the oven to 200°C/400°F/Gas Mark 6. Place 12 paper cases in a muffin tin.

Sift together the flour, baking powder and salt into a large bowl. Stir in the sugar and chocolate chunks.

Lightly beat the eggs in a large jug or bowl then beat in the milk, oil and vanilla extract.

Make a well in the centre of the dry ingredients and pour in the beaten liquid ingredients. Stir gently until just combined; do not over-mix.

Spoon the mixture into the paper cases. Bake in the preheated oven for about 20 minutes, until well risen, golden brown and firm to the touch.

Leave the muffins in the tin for 5 minutes, then serve warm or transfer to a wire rack and leave to cool.

# Blueberry Muffins

*makes 12*

280 g/10 oz plain flour

1 tbsp baking powder

⅛ tsp salt

115 g/4 oz soft light brown sugar

150 g/5½ oz frozen blueberries

2 eggs

250 ml/9 fl oz milk

6 tbsp sunflower oil or 85 g/ 3 oz butter, melted and cooled

1 tsp vanilla extract

finely grated rind of 1 lemon

Preheat the oven to 200°C/400°F/Gas Mark 6. Place 12 paper cases in a muffin tin.

Sift together the flour, baking powder and salt into a large bowl. Stir in the sugar and blueberries.

Lightly beat the eggs in a large jug or bowl then beat in the milk, oil, vanilla extract and lemon rind. Make a well in the centre of the dry ingredients and pour in the beaten liquid ingredients. Stir gently until just combined; do not over-mix.

Spoon the mixture into the paper cases. Bake in the preheated oven for about 20 minutes, until well risen, golden brown and firm to the touch.

Leave the muffins in the tin for 5 minutes, then serve warm or transfer to a wire rack and leave to cool.

# Jam Doughnut Muffins

*makes 12*

oil or melted butter,
for greasing

280 g/10 oz plain flour

1 tbsp baking powder

⅛ tsp salt

115 g/4 oz caster sugar

2 eggs

200 ml/7 fl oz milk

6 tbsp sunflower oil or 85 g/
3 oz butter, melted
and cooled

1 tsp vanilla extract

4 tbsp strawberry jam or
raspberry jam

*topping*

115 g/4 oz butter

150 g/5½ oz granulated
sugar

Preheat the oven to 200°C/400°F/Gas Mark 6. Grease a
12-cup muffin tin.

Sift together the flour, baking powder and salt into a large
bowl. Stir in the caster sugar.

Lightly beat the eggs in a large jug or bowl then beat in the
milk, oil and vanilla extract. Make a well in the centre of the
dry ingredients and pour in the beaten liquid ingredients.
Stir gently until just combined; do not over-mix.

Spoon half of the mixture into the prepared muffin tin. Add
a teaspoon of jam to the centre of each, then spoon in the
remaining mixture. Bake in the preheated oven for about
20 minutes, until well risen, golden brown and firm to
the touch.

Meanwhile, prepare the topping. Melt the butter. Spread the
granulated sugar in a wide, shallow bowl. When the muffins
are baked, leave in the tin for 5 minutes. Dip the tops of the
muffins in the melted butter then roll in the sugar. Serve
warm or transfer to a wire rack and leave to cool.

4

# Desserts

# Traditional Apple Pie

*serves 6*

*pastry*

350 g/12 oz plain flour

pinch of salt

85 g/3 oz butter or margarine, cut into small pieces

85 g/3 oz lard or white vegetable fat, cut into small pieces

beaten egg or milk, for glazing

*filling*

750 g–1 kg/1 lb 10 oz– 2 lb 4 oz cooking apples, peeled, cored and sliced

125 g/4½ oz caster sugar, plus extra for sprinkling

½–1 tsp ground cinnamon, mixed spice or ground ginger

To make the pastry, sift the flour and salt into a mixing bowl. Add the butter and lard and rub in with your fingertips until the mixture resembles fine breadcrumbs. Add about 6 tablespoons of water and gather the mixture together into a dough. Wrap the dough and chill in the refrigerator for 30 minutes.

Preheat the oven to 220°C/425°F/Gas Mark 7. Roll out almost two thirds of the pastry thinly and use to line a deep 23-cm/9-inch pie dish.

Mix the apples with the sugar and spice and pack into the pastry case; the filling can come up above the rim. Add 1–2 tablespoons of water if needed, particularly if the apples are not very juicy.

Roll out the remaining pastry to form a lid. Dampen the edges of the pie rim with water and position the lid, pressing the edges firmly together. Trim and crimp the edges.

Use the trimmings to cut out leaves or other shapes to decorate the top of the pie. Dampen and attach. Glaze the top of the pie with beaten egg, make 1–2 slits in the top and place the pie on a baking sheet.

Bake in the preheated oven for 20 minutes, then reduce the temperature to 180°C/350°F/Gas Mark 4 and bake for a further 30 minutes, or until the pastry is a light golden brown. Serve hot or cold, sprinkled with sugar.

# Forest Fruit Pie

*serves 6*

*filling*

250 g/9 oz blueberries

250 g/9 oz raspberries

250 g/9 oz blackberries

100 g/3½ oz caster sugar

*pastry*

200 g/7 oz plain flour, plus extra for dusting

25 g/1 oz ground hazelnuts

100 g/3½ oz butter, cut into small pieces, plus extra for greasing

finely grated rind of 1 lemon

1 egg yolk, beaten

4 tbsp milk

Put the berries in a saucepan with 3 tablespoons of the caster sugar and simmer, stirring frequently, for 5 minutes. Remove the pan from the heat.

Sift the flour into a bowl, then add the hazelnuts. Rub in the butter with your fingertips until the mixture resembles breadcrumbs, then stir in the remaining sugar. Add the lemon rind, egg yolk and 3 tablespoons of the milk and mix. Turn out onto a lightly floured work surface and knead briefly. Wrap and chill in the refrigerator for 30 minutes.

Preheat the oven to 190°C/375°F/Gas Mark 5. Grease a 20-cm/8-inch pie dish. Roll out two thirds of the pastry to a thickness of 5 mm/¼ inch and use it to line the dish.

Spoon the berry mixture into the pastry case. Brush the rim with water, then roll out the remaining pastry and use it to cover the pie. Trim and crimp round the edge, then make 2 small slits in the top and decorate with leaf shapes cut out from the dough trimmings. Brush all over with the remaining milk. Bake in the preheated oven for 40 minutes. Remove from the oven and serve hot.

# Rhubarb Crumble

*serves 6*

900 g/2 lb rhubarb

115 g/4 oz caster sugar

grated rind and
juice of 1 orange

*crumble topping*

225 g/8 oz plain flour

115 g/4 oz unsalted butter

115 g/4 oz soft light
brown sugar

1 tsp ground ginger

Preheat the oven to 190°C/375°F/Gas Mark 5.

Cut the rhubarb into 2.5-cm/1-inch lengths and place in a 1.7-litre/3-pint ovenproof dish with the caster sugar, orange rind and orange juice.

To make the crumble topping, place the flour in a mixing bowl and rub in the butter with your fingertips until the mixture resembles breadcrumbs. Stir in the brown sugar and ginger.

Spread the crumble topping evenly over the fruit and press down lightly using a fork. Place on a baking sheet and bake in the centre of the preheated oven for 25–30 minutes, until the topping is golden brown. Remove from the oven and serve warm.

# Blueberry Clafoutis

*serves 4*

25 g/1 oz butter, plus extra
for greasing

125 g/4½ oz caster sugar

3 eggs

60 g/2¼ oz plain flour

250 ml/9 fl oz single cream

½ tsp ground cinnamon

450 g/1 lb blueberries

icing sugar, for dusting

single cream, to serve

Preheat the oven to 180°C/350°F/Gas Mark 4. Grease a 1-litre/1¾-pint ovenproof dish.

Put the butter in a bowl with the caster sugar and whisk together until fluffy. Add the eggs and beat together well. Mix in the flour, then gradually stir in the cream followed by the cinnamon. Continue to stir until smooth.

Arrange the blueberries in the base of the prepared dish, then pour over the batter. Transfer to the preheated oven and bake for about 30 minutes, or until puffed and golden.

Remove from the oven, dust lightly with icing sugar and serve with cream.

# Tarte au Citron

*serves 6–8*

grated rind of
2–3 large lemons

150 ml/5 fl oz lemon juice

100 g/3½ oz caster sugar

125 ml/4 fl oz double cream
or crème fraîche

3 large eggs

3 large egg yolks

icing sugar, for dusting

fresh raspberries, to serve

*pastry*

175 g/6 oz plain flour, plus
extra for dusting

½ tsp salt

115 g/4 oz cold unsalted
butter, diced

1 egg yolk, beaten with
2 tbsp ice-cold water

To make the pastry, sift the flour and salt into a large bowl. Add the butter and rub it in with your fingertips until the mixture resembles fine breadcrumbs. Add the egg yolk and water and stir to mix to a dough. Gather the dough into a ball, wrap in clingfilm and leave to chill for at least 1 hour.

Preheat the oven to 200°C/400°F/Gas Mark 6. Roll the dough out on a lightly floured work surface and use to line a 23–25-cm/9–10-inch loose-based tart tin. Prick the base of the pastry all over with a fork and line with baking paper and baking beans.

Bake in the preheated oven for 15 minutes, until the pastry looks set. Remove the paper and beans. Reduce the oven temperature to 190°C/375°F/Gas Mark 5.

Beat the lemon rind, lemon juice and caster sugar together until blended. Slowly beat in the cream, then beat in the eggs and yolks, one by one.

Place the pastry case on a baking sheet and pour in the filling. Transfer to the preheated oven and bake for 20 minutes, until the filling is set.

Leave to cool completely on a wire rack. Dust with icing sugar and serve with raspberries.

# Spiced Apple Tart

*serves 6–8*

*pastry*

200 g/7 oz plain flour, plus extra for dusting

100 g/3½ oz butter, diced, plus extra for greasing

50 g/1¾ oz icing sugar, sifted

finely grated rind of 1 lemon

1 egg yolk, beaten

3 tbsp milk

*filling*

3 cooking apples

2 tbsp lemon juice

finely grated rind of 1 lemon

150 ml/5 fl oz honey

175 g/6 oz fresh white or wholemeal breadcrumbs

1 tsp mixed spice

pinch of ground nutmeg

To make the pastry, sift the flour into a bowl. Rub in the butter, then mix in the icing sugar, lemon rind, egg yolk and milk. Knead briefly, then wrap in clingfilm and chill in the refrigerator for 30 minutes.

Preheat the oven to 200°C/400°F/Gas Mark 6. Grease a 20-cm/8-inch tart tin. Roll out the pastry to a thickness of 5 mm/¼ inch and use to line the tin.

To make the filling, core 2 of the apples and grate them into a bowl. Add 1 tablespoon of the lemon juice and all the lemon rind, along with the honey, breadcrumbs and mixed spice. Mix together well. Spoon evenly into the pastry case.

Core and slice the remaining apple, and use to decorate the top of the tart. Brush the apple slices with the remaining lemon juice, then sprinkle over the nutmeg.

Bake in the preheated oven for 35 minutes, or until firm. Remove from the oven and serve warm.

# Chestnut, Maple Syrup & Pecan Tart

*serves 6*

*pastry*

125 g/4½ oz plain flour, plus extra for dusting

pinch of salt

75 g/3 oz cold butter, cut into pieces, plus extra for greasing

*filling*

1 kg/2 lb 4 oz canned sweetened chestnut purée

300 ml/10 fl oz double cream

25 g/1 oz butter

2 tbsp maple syrup

150 g/5½ oz pecan nuts

Grease a 23-cm/9-inch loose-based fluted tart tin. Sift the flour and salt into a food processor, add the butter and process until the mixture resembles fine breadcrumbs. Tip the mixture into a large bowl and add a little cold water, just enough to bring the dough together.

Turn out onto a lightly floured work surface and roll out the pastry 8 cm/3¼ inches larger than the tin. Carefully lift the pastry into the tin and press to fit. Roll the rolling pin over the tin to neaten the edges and trim the excess pastry. Fit a piece of baking paper into the tart case, fill with baking beans and chill in the refrigerator for 30 minutes. Meanwhile, preheat the oven to 190°C/ 375°F/Gas Mark 5.

Remove the pastry case from the refrigerator and bake in the preheated oven for 15 minutes, then remove the beans and paper and bake for a further 10 minutes.

Empty the chestnut purée into a large bowl. Whip the cream until stiff and fold into the chestnut purée. Spoon into the cold pastry case and chill for 2 hours.

Melt the butter with the maple syrup and when bubbling add the pecans and stir for 1–2 minutes. Spoon onto baking paper and cool. When ready to serve, arrange the pecans on the chestnut cream.

# Chocolate Truffle Torte

*serves 10*

butter, for greasing

50 g/1¾ oz caster sugar

2 eggs

40 g/1½ oz plain flour

25 g/1 oz cocoa powder

4 tbsp strong black coffee

2 tbsp brandy

cocoa powder and icing sugar, for dusting

*truffle filling*

600 ml/1 pint whipping cream

425 g/15 oz plain chocolate, broken into pieces

Preheat the oven to 220°C/425°F/Gas Mark 7. Grease a 23-cm/9-inch round cake tin and line with baking paper.

Put the sugar and eggs in a heatproof bowl set over a saucepan of gently simmering water. Whisk together until pale and resembling the texture of mousse. Sift in the flour and cocoa and fold gently into the mixture. Pour into the prepared tin and bake in the preheated oven for 7–10 minutes, or until risen and firm to the touch.

Transfer to a wire rack to cool. Wash and dry the tin and replace the cooled cake in the tin. Mix together the coffee and brandy and brush over the cake.

To make the truffle filling, put the cream in a bowl and whisk until just holding very soft peaks. Put the chocolate in a heatproof bowl set over a saucepan of gently simmering water until melted. Carefully fold the cooled melted chocolate into the cream. Pour the chocolate mixture over the sponge. Chill until set.

To decorate the torte, sift cocoa over the top and remove carefully from the tin. Using strips of baking paper, sift bands of icing sugar over the torte to create a striped pattern. Cut into slices with a hot knife.

# Ricotta Cheesecake

*serves 6–8*

*pastry*

175 g/6 oz plain flour, plus extra for dusting

3 tbsp caster sugar

pinch of salt

115 g/4 oz unsalted butter, chilled and diced

1 egg yolk

*filling*

450 g/1 lb ricotta cheese

125 ml/4 fl oz double cream

2 eggs, plus 1 egg yolk

85 g/3 oz caster sugar

finely grated rind of 1 lemon

finely grated rind of 1 orange

To make the pastry, sift the flour with the sugar and salt onto a work surface and make a well in the centre. Add the diced butter and egg yolk to the well and, using your fingertips, gradually work into the flour mixture until fully incorporated.

Gather up the dough and knead very lightly. Cut off about one quarter, wrap in clingfilm and chill in the refrigerator. Press the remaining dough into the base of a 23-cm/9-inch loose-based tart tin. Chill for 30 minutes. Meanwhile, preheat the oven to 190°C/375°F/Gas Mark 5.

To make the filling, beat the ricotta cheese with the cream, eggs and extra egg yolk, sugar, lemon rind and orange rind. Cover with clingfilm and place in the refrigerator until required.

Prick the base of the pastry case all over with a fork. Line with baking paper, fill with baking beans and bake in the preheated oven for 15 minutes.

Remove the pastry case from the oven and take out the baking paper and beans. Stand the tin on a wire rack and set aside to cool. Spoon the ricotta mixture into the pastry case and smooth the surface. Roll out the reserved pastry on a lightly floured surface and cut it into strips. Arrange the strips over the filling in a lattice pattern, brushing the overlapping ends with water so that they stick.

Bake for a further 30–35 minutes, until the top of the cheesecake is golden and the filling has set. Cool on a wire rack before removing from the tin.

# Manhattan Cheesecake

*serves 8–10*

sunflower oil, for brushing

85 g/3 oz butter

200 g/7 oz digestive biscuits, crushed

400 g/14 oz cream cheese

2 large eggs

140 g/5 oz caster sugar

1½ tsp vanilla extract

450 ml/16 fl oz soured cream

*blueberry topping*

55 g/2 oz caster sugar

4 tbsp water

250 g/9 oz fresh blueberries

1 tsp arrowroot

Preheat the oven to 190°C/375°F/Gas Mark 5. Brush a 20-cm/8-inch springform round cake tin with oil.

Melt the butter in a saucepan over a low heat. Stir in the biscuits, then spread over the base of the tin.

Place the cream cheese, eggs, 100 g/3½ oz of the sugar and ½ teaspoon of the vanilla extract in a food processor. Process until smooth. Pour over the biscuit base and smooth the top. Place on a baking sheet and bake in the preheated oven for 20 minutes, until set. Remove from the oven and leave for 20 minutes. Leave the oven switched on.

Mix the soured cream with the remaining sugar and vanilla extract in a bowl. Spoon over the cheesecake. Return it to the oven for 10 minutes, leave to cool, then cover with clingfilm and chill in the refrigerator for 8 hours, or overnight.

To make the topping, place the sugar in a saucepan with 2 tablespoons of the water over a low heat and stir until the sugar has dissolved. Increase the heat, add the blueberries, cover and cook for a few minutes, or until they begin to soften. Remove from the heat. Mix the arrowroot and remaining water in a bowl, add to the blueberries and stir until smooth. Return to a low heat. Cook until the juice thickens and turns translucent. Leave to cool.

Remove the cheesecake from the tin 1 hour before serving. Spoon over the blueberry topping and chill until ready to serve.

# Chocolate Brownie Roulade

*serves 6*

butter, for greasing

150 g/5½ oz plain chocolate, broken into pieces

3 tbsp water

175 g/6 oz caster sugar

5 eggs, separated

25 g/1 oz raisins, chopped

25 g/1 oz pecan nuts, chopped

pinch of salt

icing sugar, for dusting

300 ml/10 fl oz double cream, lightly whipped

Preheat the oven to 180°C/350°F/Gas Mark 4. Grease a 30 x 20-cm/12 x 8-inch Swiss roll tin and line with baking paper.

Melt the chocolate with the water in a small saucepan over a low heat until the chocolate has melted. Leave to cool.

In a bowl, whisk the sugar and egg yolks for 2–3 minutes with a hand-held electric whisk until thick and pale. Fold in the cooled chocolate, raisins and pecan nuts.

In a separate bowl, whisk the egg whites with the salt. Fold one quarter of the egg whites into the chocolate mixture, then fold in the rest of the whites, working lightly and quickly.

Transfer the mixture to the prepared tin and bake in the preheated oven for 25 minutes, until risen and just firm to the touch. Leave to cool before covering with a sheet of baking paper and a damp clean tea towel. Leave until cold.

Turn the roulade out onto another piece of baking paper dusted with icing sugar and carefully remove the lining paper.

Spread the cream over the roulade. Starting from a short end, roll the sponge away from you using the paper to guide you. Trim the ends of the roulade to make a neat finish and transfer to a serving plate. Leave to chill in the refrigerator. Dust with icing sugar before serving.

# Peach Melba Meringue Roulade

*serves 8*

sunflower oil, for brushing

*coulis*

350 g/12 oz fresh raspberries

115 g/4 oz icing sugar

*meringue*

2 tsp cornflour

300 g/10½ oz caster sugar

5 large egg whites

1 tsp cider vinegar

*filling*

3 peaches, peeled, stoned and chopped

250 g/9 oz fresh raspberries

200 ml/7 fl oz crème fraîche

150 ml/5 fl oz double cream

Preheat the oven to 150°C/300°F/Gas Mark 2. Brush a 35 x 25-cm/14 x 10-inch Swiss roll tin with oil and line with baking paper.

To make the coulis, process the raspberries and icing sugar to a purée. Press through a sieve into a bowl and reserve.

To make the meringue, sift the cornflour into a bowl and stir in the sugar. In a separate, spotlessly clean bowl, whisk the egg whites into stiff peaks, then whisk in the vinegar. Gradually whisk in the cornflour and sugar mixture until stiff and glossy.

Spread the mixture evenly in the prepared tin, leaving a 1-cm/½-inch border. Bake in the centre of the preheated oven for 20 minutes, then reduce the heat to 110°C/225°F/Gas Mark ¼ and cook for a further 25–30 minutes, or until puffed up. Remove from the oven. Leave to cool for 15 minutes. Turn out onto another piece of baking paper and carefully remove the lining paper.

To make the filling, place the peaches in a bowl with the raspberries. Add 2 tablespoons of the coulis and mix. In a separate bowl, whisk the crème fraîche and cream together until thick. Spread over the meringue. Scatter the fruit over the cream, leaving a 3-cm/1¼-inch border at one short edge. Using the baking paper, lift and roll the meringue, starting at the short edge without the border, ending up seam-side down. Lift onto a plate and serve with the coulis.

# Strawberry Shortcake

*serves 8*

175 g/6 oz self-raising flour

100 g/3½ oz unsalted butter, diced and chilled, plus extra for greasing

75 g/2¾ oz caster sugar

1 egg yolk

1 tbsp rosewater

600 ml/1 pint whipping cream, lightly whipped

225 g/8 oz strawberries, hulled and quartered, plus a few whole strawberries to decorate

icing sugar, for dusting

Preheat the oven to 190°C/375°F/Gas Mark 5. Grease two baking sheets and line with baking paper.

To make the shortcakes, sift the flour into a bowl. Rub in the butter with your fingers until the mixture resembles breadcrumbs. Stir in the sugar, then add the egg yolk and rosewater and mix to form a soft dough.

Divide the dough in half. Roll out each piece into a 19-cm/7½-inch round and transfer each one to a prepared baking sheet. Crimp the edges of the dough and prick all over with a fork.

Bake in the preheated oven for 15 minutes, until lightly golden. Transfer the shortcakes to a wire rack to cool.

Mix the cream with the strawberry quarters and spoon on top of one of the shortcakes. Cut the remaining shortcake round into wedges, then place on top of the cream. Dust with icing sugar and decorate with whole strawberries.

# Raspberry Dessert Cake

*serves 10*

225 g/8 oz butter, plus extra for greasing

250 g/9 oz plain chocolate

1 tbsp strong black coffee

5 eggs

90 g/3¼ oz golden caster sugar

90 g/3¼ oz plain flour, sifted

1 tsp ground cinnamon

150 g/5½ oz fresh raspberries, plus extra to serve

cocoa powder, for dusting

whipped cream, to serve

Preheat the oven to 160°C/325°F/Gas Mark 3. Grease a 23-cm/9-inch round cake tin and line with baking paper.

Put the butter, chocolate and coffee in a heatproof bowl set over a saucepan of gently simmering water and heat until melted. Stir and leave to cool slightly.

Put the eggs and sugar in a bowl and beat until thick and pale. Gently fold in the chocolate mixture. Sift the flour and cinnamon into a bowl, then fold into the chocolate mixture. Pour into the prepared tin and sprinkle the raspberries evenly over the top.

Bake in the preheated oven for 35–45 minutes, until the cake is well risen and springy to the touch. Leave to cool in the tin for 15 minutes before turning out onto a large plate. Dust with cocoa and serve with raspberries and whipped cream.

# Almond & Hazelnut Gateau

*serves 8*

butter, for greasing

4 eggs

115 g/4 oz caster sugar

50 g/1¾ oz ground almonds

50 g/1¾ oz ground hazelnuts

50 g/1¾ oz plain flour

70 g/2½ oz flaked almonds

icing sugar, for dusting

*filling*

100 g/3½ oz plain chocolate, broken into pieces

1 tbsp butter

300 ml/10 fl oz double cream

Preheat the oven to 190°C/375°F/Gas Mark 5. Grease two 18-cm/7-inch sandwich tins and line with baking paper.

Whisk the eggs and caster sugar in a large mixing bowl with an electric whisk for about 10 minutes, or until the mixture is very light and foamy and a trail is left when the whisk is dragged across the surface.

Fold in the ground nuts. Sift the flour and fold in with a metal spoon or palette knife. Divide the mixture between the prepared tins.

Scatter the flaked almonds over the top of one of the cakes. Bake both of the cakes in the preheated oven for 15–20 minutes, or until springy to the touch.

Leave to cool slightly in the tins. Remove the cakes from the tins and transfer to a wire rack to cool completely. Meanwhile, make the filling. Melt the chocolate in a heatproof bowl set over a saucepan of gently simmering water, remove from the heat and stir in the butter. Leave the mixture to cool slightly. Whip the cream until just holding its shape, then fold in the melted chocolate mixture.

Place the cake without the extra almonds on a serving plate and spread the filling over it. Leave the filling to set slightly, then place the almond-topped cake on top and chill for about 1 hour. Dust with icing sugar and serve.

# Sticky Toffee Cake

*serves 4*

75 g/2¾ oz sultanas

150 g/5½ oz stoned dates, chopped

1 tsp bicarbonate of soda

25 g/1 oz butter, plus extra for greasing

200 g/7 oz soft dark brown sugar

2 eggs

200 g/7 oz self-raising flour, sifted

*sticky toffee sauce*

25 g/1 oz butter

175 ml/6 fl oz double cream

200 g/7 oz soft dark brown sugar

Put the sultanas, dates and bicarbonate of soda into a heatproof bowl. Cover with boiling water and leave to soak.

Preheat the oven to 180°C/350°F/Gas Mark 4. Grease a 18-cm/7-inch square cake tin. Put the butter in a separate bowl, add the sugar and mix well. Beat in the eggs then fold in the flour. Drain the soaked fruits, add to the bowl and mix.

Spoon the mixture evenly into the prepared cake tin. Transfer to the preheated oven and bake for 35–40 minutes, or until a skewer inserted into the centre comes out clean.

About 5 minutes before the end of the cooking time, make the sauce. Melt the butter in a saucepan over a medium heat. Stir in the cream and sugar and bring to the boil, stirring constantly. Lower the heat and simmer for 5 minutes.

Cut the cake into squares and turn out onto serving plates. Pour over the sauce and serve.

# Profiteroles

serves 4

**choux pastry**

70 g/2½ oz unsalted butter, plus extra for greasing

200 ml/7 fl oz water

100 g/3½ oz plain flour

3 eggs, beaten

**cream filling**

300 ml/10 fl oz double cream

3 tbsp caster sugar

1 tsp vanilla extract

**chocolate & brandy sauce**

125 g/4½ oz plain chocolate, broken into small pieces

35 g/1¼ oz unsalted butter

6 tbsp water

2 tbsp brandy

Preheat the oven to 200°C/400°F/Gas Mark 6. Grease a large baking sheet.

To make the pastry, place the butter and water in a saucepan and bring to the boil. Meanwhile, sift the flour into a bowl. Turn off the heat and beat in the flour until smooth. Cool for 5 minutes. Beat in enough of the eggs to give the mixture a soft dropping consistency.

Transfer to a piping bag fitted with a 1-cm/½-inch plain nozzle. Pipe small balls onto the prepared baking sheet. Bake in the preheated oven for 25 minutes.

Remove from the oven. Pierce each ball with a skewer to let the steam escape.

To make the filling, whip the cream, sugar and vanilla extract together. Cut the pastry balls across the centre, then fill with cream.

To make the sauce, gently melt the chocolate, butter and water together in a small saucepan, stirring constantly, until smooth. Stir in the brandy. Pile the profiteroles into individual serving dishes, pour over the sauce and serve.